To:
_____
With love from:
_____

I Celebrate You, Daughter!

Michelle Allen

COUNTRYMAN

Copyright © 2000 by Michelle Allen

Published by J. Countryman
a division of Thomas Nelson, Inc., Nashville, Tennessee 37214

Project Editor - Terri Gibbs

Designed by Starletta Polster, Murfreesboro, Tennessee

ISBN: 0-8499-5773-7

www.jcountryman.com

Printed in China

A thing of beauty is a joy forever.
John Keats

Allen

You are:
My little girl forever,
my joy forever.

Here are some of

the wonderfully unique things

I cherish about you:

_____

_____

_____

_____

_____

_____

CHeRiSH FOReVeR WHAT Makes YOU UNiQue

Allen

How many times
you have shown me...

What a wonderful heart
you have!

There is always

joy and sunshine

in the heart

that beats with

kindness.

You're the kind
of daughter
I'm so glad
to have.

Love is its own reward.
~Thomas Merton~

To love
and be
loved is
the
greatest
happiness
in life.

You bring happiness

to others by

_____

_____

_____

_____

_____

There is only one just like you in the whole world.

No one
makes the world
a better place
quite
like you do.

A smiling heart spreads flowers
along life's way.

©Allen

A daughter like you
makes all
the difference.

This is just one way
you have made a
difference in my life.

_____

_____

_____

_____

_____

Be all that God created you
to be.

If you think
you can,
you can.
If you want
to,
you will.

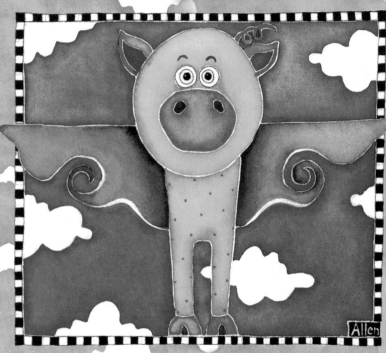

I think you're terrific!

You deserve a

standing ovation for

_____

_____

_____

_____

_____

_____

Every good and

perfect gift

is from above.

James 1:17

I'm so glad God gave
you to me.
Without you...
how boring and empty
my life would be!

This is my prayer
for you dearest daughter:

_____

_____

_____

_____

_____

_____

_____

_____

I'm so glad
you are you.
Be silly or
sophisticated,
wacky or cool,
but always be you!